Of

Infinite

Simplicity

A

Guide

For

Homeless

Meditation Practitioners

By Kiley Jon Clark

To my beloved Guru and Perfect Teacher, Lama Tulku Tsori Rinpoche, the Great-Being who builds Monasteries in desolate places for orphan refugee children and causes them to prosper with Pure Motivation and Diamond-like Intent.

May he receive innumerable blessings and offerings to help fund his Humanitarian Effort, of training young monks and nuns to carry the message of encouragement, non-violence, patience, loving-kindness, and generosity, to the far flung corners of this Earth. (YTDR.org)

To the author of Lojong's root text, Geshe Chekawa, the Buddhist Saint who lived in a Leper Colony and taught daily the practice of Tonglen & Lojong. Because of his heartfelt devotion, many people suffering from leprosy were given back their lives, and those without leprosy learned the true meaning of compassion.

Lastly, to my Homeless Brothers and Sisters around the World, those living in the streets, parks, campsites, alleys, under bridges, pay-per-week motels, shelters, jails, institutions, and even in huge mansions. There is a purpose for your life.

Kiley Jon Clark
Sonam Gyatso
(Ocean of Merit)

Written in a Texas Courtyard for the Homeless
On the Night before the Full moon
March 7, 2012

"My mind is the perfect Buddha,
My speech the perfect Dharma,
My body the perfect Sangha,
There is no need to search for Naropa...
'I Am' here!"

– Non-duality Song of Marpa's Guru

FOREWORD

by kiley jon clark

After years of doing meditation on the streets, under bridges, and in shelters within the Homeless Community…this message happened through me…it was not of my doing…and it has an Energy of its own…waiting to change the consciousness of both the Householder and the Homeless alike…if we listen.

Yes, this message is for everyone, including you. But it specifically needs to get into the hands of those living on the streets…living without hope, not even knowing that they, like us, are part of a Noble, Sacred Tradition.

The Non-Duality Teachings that appear in this text are more than Ancient…they come from a State of Mind where neither time, nor a self to experience time, exists. It is not a place you can go, only a place you can be. So, sit back and smile…you're already home.

Prayer:

May this text be of some benefit to all Beings,

Whom…are none other than my own Self.

By putting these teachings into practice,

May we seek within and see…

There truly is no separation between us, no separation

From love, no separation from God or Buddha-Nature,

No death, no suffering, no you, no me,

And all there ever was or will be…is the SOURCE

…of these illusionary thoughts.

1

Fault With Others

Everything is Eternal

But Nothing Lasts.

There is no Death,

Only Transformation.

Depression is the fatigue
Of holding on.

It is one blink from
The Bliss of Letting Go.

Oh Seeker, Listen!

You are not alone.
It is an ancient Tradition.

From time without beginning,
Holy Men and Sacred Women
Have gone forth Into Homelessness.

To wander,
In Search of Truth,
They go.

They have stepped out of society
And themselves,
Seeking
The Mind-Which-Is-Free-From-Doubt.

Alone or within a Community,
For the Good of all Humanity,
They have renounced the World.

Up into the Mountains,
Deep in the Forest,
Down the Road,
And hidden in plain sight,
They have Crossed the Stream.

Many are the brave men and courageous women
Who have followed
The example of our Perfect Teacher,
Siddhartha,
Into the Homeless life.

For he, although only human,
Was able to conquer himself
And Awaken the Body of Formlessness.

Troubled and burdened by life,
Siddhartha walked away
From the responsibilities of royalty
And the expectations of wealth.

How strong he must have been,
To trade it all in and disappear
Into that lonely night.

How it broke his heart,
To turn his back on his father, stepmother,
Wife, and newborn son.

But he realized that all beings,
Including his wife and son
Would eventually suffer old-age,
Sickness, and demise.

So, with only a begging bowl
And determination,
He set out to understand
This mystery called,
"Birth and Death"
And find a Way that leads to
The end of Sorrow.

As many have done before him
And the countless ones still to come,
This poor-homeless-one-meal-a-day
-Eating-vagabond-Siddhartha,
 Awoke from his sleep,
Entered into his Enlightenment,
And became a "Buddha"!

Because of his determination, pure motivation,
And endless compassion, he escaped worldly bondage.

Straight away he departed,
Walking over two hundred miles
To preach his very first sermon
To five homeless friends, thus
 Releasing them from the trap of suffering,
That he himself had been caught in.

This turning of the Wheel of Teaching,
Is still releasing Beings from the
Same cycle of sadness, loneliness,
And heartache today.

His quest being won and the prize attained
He was able to return to his Kingdom,
Although not as himself,
But as that which survives old-age,
Sickness, and Death!

Lovingly and tenderly, he led his father,
 Step-mother, wife, and son
Onto the Raft of Wisdom
That crosses the Ocean of Suffering.

But Oh Seeker,
Of the Buddha Siddhartha
And all his accomplishments
We could read volumes!

Talking endlessly about
How he found the Water of Enlightenment
Cannot quench our own thirst…
We must go to the Well ourselves.

So, what about you,
Oh Great-Being?

Are you ready to push off toward the Other Shore
Or do you still mistake this ragged,
Bag of bones for a home?

Tell me,
Who are the Homeless
And who are the Housed?

Can you show me, even one creature
That has found a permanent home here?

Who is there among us, that is not
Endlessly migrating from body to body,
Life to life, repeatedly landing
In deeper planes of suffering?

By Ignorance of our true Nature,
All beings have been
Cast out of Wisdom.

But there is a doorway back,
And there are those who have found it.

They are the "Great Renouncers".

They have left the world to wander...
In truth, beauty, and bliss.

Some have renounced in mind and body,
To become the Goodness of the Street.

Others have renounced in their Hearts,
To become the Goodness of Society.

To the first, a retreat from all obligations is needed
For the Spiritual Work of freeing all Beings.

To the second, immersion in obligation,
Commerce, and family is the very path
To Awakening the World.

Oh Seeker,
Live as you like,
Whether as a Monk, Nun,
Practitioner, or MahaSiddha,
But be honorable. Be purposeful.

Be homeless in spirit, without attachment.

Respect the Ancient, Unbroken
Chain of Great Renouncers.

Respect the lineage of those men and women
Who won their freedom
By seeing themselves in All-Beings
 Until they became All-Beings.

Respect the Crazy Wisdom Tradition of those Homeless Saints
Who were able to cut the net and fly to heaven.

They left behind a trail for us to follow
Into that Great-Bliss-Union
Of our own Buddha-Nature.

So, whether Homeless in Body and Mind
Or Homeless in the Heart,
Be brothers and sisters
Of the Way.

See yourself in each other.
Champion your Ego.
Know that all Beings are you
 Under different circumstances.

Visualize the needs of all Beings
As being met,
And then set a relaxed hand
To making it happen.

Remember:
You have to be "nowhere"
You have to be "nothing"

You are the Emptiness of fire,
Water, earth, and wind.

You are well, happy, content,
In need of nothing
And helpful
To every living thing.

You know that,
Goodness attracts Goodness.
Kindness attracts Kindness.
Generosity attracts Generosity.

It is an Inexhaustible Law,
That in which,
You dwell upon,
Talk and think about,
Is what you become.

As a Brick-Layer rebuilds a wall,
Brick by brick,
Reconstruct the World
Thought by thought.

See it with your imagination,
And work for it
With your hand.

Oh Seeker,
How extremely rare, this opportunity!

You have been born a human with
The ability and leisure
To free yourself and others
From this bondage of negative thought.

You are free. You are the mist. You are the distant Rainbow.
Your mind is the Great, Expansive Sky!
You are the Body of Infinite Simplicity
Within which Whirls
The entire Living Cosmos.

2

Unbearable Fire-Bowl

Question your "self."
Where are your riches now?

Where is your reward
For so many lives
Spent chasing Praise
And Gain?

Oh, the many
Houses you have owned.
All blown away
As dust, by now.

Oh, the blushing brides
And distinguished husbands
You have had.
All blown away
As dust, by now.

And, why even speak
Of all the mothers,
Fathers, and children
You have had?

How many loved ones
Have let go of your hand
And fallen into the grave
During these countless lifetimes?

Remember,
You beat your chest
And screamed that you would never forget?

But, how can you say that you remember any of them now,
When you don't even remember your own many deaths?

Imposter! Master of disguise!

More numerable than the garments
Sold by a rich Merchant,
Oh the various bodies
You yourself have recklessly worn
And discarded!

All blown away
As dust, by now.

Time laughs at such
Unimportant things.
And are you
Still clinging?

Do you still mistake
This tired bag
Of guts for you?

Perhaps this question can rattle around
In a cage of bones,
But the answer can never be trapped
Behind these bars lined with meat!

Oh Seeker, life is so much
More than the body!

But, how confusing,
This Mind of Trickery,
It goes on solidifying itself even in sleep.

Thoughts spontaneously
Rise and fall like stormy waves
In an Ocean of fear, regret, and hope.

Seeking rest, Oh Great-Being,
Do not look in the distance
For what is already in front of you.

Go into the gap between thoughts.

Seeing there,
No more of this fantasy
Called, "Myself Alone".

This nagging
Chain of fear, shyness,
Terror, timidity,
And self-pity is broken.

You are free.
There is nothing that binds you
Except your own thoughts.

You are the invisible expanse of Universe.
Don't trade this immeasurable Vastness,
For a puny, false-self!

A fool trades a sack of gold
For a sack of dirt,
Because the dirt
Is more familiar to him!

Look at the World,
Look into the darkness within,
Do you find a "Self"?

You are awake
In a world that is dreaming.

Patiently help those
Who still struggle.

Like a lion leaping out of its cage,
The Body of Infinite Simplicity
Is free to act in huge,
Miraculous Ways!

3

Dungeon Dark

It is easy
To stay asleep,
Dwelling
In delusion.

Take a breath.

Spy on the Present Moment until
It becomes Brilliant Light.

Everything is within your grasp,
But not graspable.

Nothing remains, yet here it is
Self-Luminous.

A million, blurred days,
And are you still
Racing?

You have become blind.
See again, without judgment.

What is "Night"?
What is "Sunlight"?
What is "your Name"?
What is "your current address"?
Who could possibly know such wondrous things?

What use is all this talk about
"Like" and "Dislike",
"Yesterday",
"Today" and "Tomorrow"?

There is no way of holding on
To these things…by naming them!

The clock never moves.
There are no pages on the calendar.
Look around, eternity is now.

Be aware only
Of the Great-Bliss-Energy-Of-Emptiness,
And them that dwell blindly within it.

Things are neither real nor unreal,
So never have more then you need.

Whatever "is"
Is a distraction.

Give it all away.

When your current mind sees "lack"
It creates "need".

When your current mind sees "problem"
It worries and frets over "solution".

Let it be!

The power of thought is strong.
Use this incredible imagination wisely.

As you Breath-In deeply,
Visualize the pain and suffering
That the world seems to feel.

As you Breath-Out completely,
Visualize the pure, sweet,
Golden-Light of prosperity, healing,
Companionship, freedom and
Peace that the world seems to need.

This activity is called, "Tonglen" or
Taking and Giving Mediation.

It is now,
Your daily Practice.

Trust that it will train your mind
And guide your hand.

4

Swamp of Three Poisons

Difficult indeed,
It is to be born
A Human!

Have you been born
An animal so many times
That you still want to
Act like one?

Fighting, eating, sleeping,
Shitting, urinating and protecting the "Self"
What creature doesn't do this already?

Come on, Awaken!
Lose the fear.

Rows of Razor Sharp Teeth,
Arrows and Knives have never
Killed what you truly are.

Being Human is your only chance to
Go beyond Birth and Death.

Be of benefit to others, and Shine!

Happiness, Sadness,
Suffering and Joy
Are all Mind-Produced.

So, let go of Anger,
Jealously, Depression,
And Worry.

All these tiresome thoughts
Are like being chased
In a dream.

When you awaken,
There is nothing to fear.

Step Back.
Open Your Heart.
Breathe Deeply into the Chest.

Choose your Thoughts.
Choose your Emotions.

Have you not grown weary
Of pointing a crooked finger
At the World and yelling,
"Change! Change!"?

It will not, but you will.
And by your changing, it changes.

Oh, Great Being,
Be Happy.

Whatever you think of the World,
It thinks of you.

Negative or Positive,
It rebounds upon you.

So, be Patient.
Be Gentle.
Hold your Tongue.

Ask yourself,
"What is it that is born?"
"What is it that dies?"

Although completely without substance,
Something appears
To be born, but where does it come from?

Although completely without substance,
Something appears
To die, but where does it go?

Since this something is really nothing that
Can ever be described,
It will never satisfy your expectations.

Buddha Siddhartha taught on "Emptiness"
So that his monks and nuns
Would quit being so grumpy,
Miserly with their attention,
And spendthrift with their kindness!

Oh Great-Being,
See how all negative-thought
Causes only further Suffering?

Around and Around
We have gone,
Too numerous to count,
Arguing, protecting, worrying, and hording.

Aren't you tired, yet?

Look at your life.
Choose how to Live.
Give it all Away.

Let go of this,
And not only this,
But even more.

Be Free.

Don't try too hard,
But don't procrastinate.

Make all of your actions,
Virtuous and Joyous.

Remain in a state of alert awareness,
Seeing the intimate details of the Moment.

Know that you can never be separated,
Even for a moment, from the Body of Infinite Simplicity.

You are dreaming this world and the "Self"
That is experiencing it.

In your life you will see wealth, fame, honor, respect,
Sickness, starvation, injury, disease, brutal attacks, senseless
Deaths and many other Blissful things...

These are all created
 With your own thoughts.

Go beyond doubt.

Inhale:
The broke-down, defeated tortured life.
Exhale:
A beneficial Universe that so eagerly helps you at every turn.

By this Practice,
Much change will occur.

5

The Fearful Wave

The Electric Drumbeat
In the Center of your Chest,
Feeds All the Rest.

Your Heartbeat is interconnected
To the Pulse of Everything,
Seen and Unseen.

Give it use of your eyes,
Ears, tongue, touch, and mind.

Breathe into the Chest, Deeply.

See with your Heart.

Visualize that the heart is a wheel
Shooting rainbow light beams
Throughout all the Worlds
As it spins around and around!

These rays of Light are liberating
All Beings from their suffering.

Oh Great-Being,
Think only of the Happiness of others.

Wish for them,
All you could ever want for yourself.
All knowledge, All matter,

All thought, All energy,
All that ever was, or ever will be,
Is here now.

Your only work,
Is to find that it is you,
 Living and breathing in all things.

Hold a vision of all creatures being
Free from poverty, danger,
 Illness, addiction, worry, heartache, fear and doubt.

Make this your heart's desire.
Hold this image steadfast in your mind,
See it over and over.

Enter into your imagination.

See that all Beings are already perfect in health,
Safe, blessed, prosperous, and loved.

See it clearly, again and again.

Stir up a feeling within yourself, that this wish
Is already accomplished and rejoice!

This is the Teaching of all the Buddhas
And all Enlightened Masters
Past and future.
It is still being preached
In the Silence
Between Heartbeats.

6

Spider's Web

See the World
As a Jeweled Kingdom,
And Every Creature
As Divinity.

Believe that everything is conscious
And affected by thought.

Breath-In: The forced sickness, neglect, atrocity, confusion,
And stupidity of our blood-drenched history of war…with its
  Battlefields of Insanity.

Breath-Out: Rays of Wisdom, healing, comfort, kindness,
Clear-thinking, compassion, and Love, with the hope that we can
  Make peace swiftly…
Even before the argument.

There are only two kinds of words and actions.

Seek those things which are beneficial and bring
Happiness and leave that which is unbeneficial
And brings only further Suffering.

Make peace with your World.
Be Grateful for everything.

Let the Heart of Goodness decide
  The proper response
And action in all matters.

Get away from so much
"I like" and "I dislike".

Let down your armor of anxiety.

Look within.
Follow your Heart.

Do no Harm,
And see.

See all Beings as Perfect Mothers.

Pretend that all Beings love us deeply
And care for us completely!

This is not a weakness, on the contrary,
It is your biggest strength.

As people are treated, they act accordingly.

By what Beings want the most,
The environment is transformed.

Show reverence to everything.
Treat each atom as a Wish-Granting Jewel!

All creatures are Perfect Mother-Beings
Without whom,
We would be alone, naked, and hungry!

Just look at your clothes,
Who knows how many Beings
Worked hard, were injured, or even died
Putting that one garment together?

Look at each plate of food.

How many animals, insects,
And other creatures were affected
In the production of this food?

Be grateful for every little thing.

Every single speck of dust
In the sunlight,
Is a glowing jewel on Indra's Net,
Helping you see clearly enough
To Awaken.

7

Fowler's Net

This World is hard enough without projecting
Imagined insult and injury.

You are not the Master,
Or the Servant, so remain
Comfortably indifferent.

There is no end to distractions.

Life barges in,
Even in a Retreat Cave.

Be Calm.
Embrace the World.

Work with what
Spontaneously Arises in the Mind.

Why be scared
Of the echo,
When it is you
Making the Sound?

Aspire to create
Happiness in all those around you.

The World is a Magical Mirror,
It reflects back your own thoughts.

Thinking, "The World is awful!"
It will rise only to displease you.

Thinking, "The World is wonderful!"
It will rise only to please you.

Perfect-Being,
Everything, in its natural state,
Is crystal clear and simple.

The Body of Infinite Simplicity
Looks into the Mirror
And sees nothing.

And are you still showing the Mirror,
"I Need",
"I Hope",
"I Wish",
And "I hate myself!"?

You can't fool a Mirror,
Only yourself.

You can't change a Mirror,
Only yourself.

When you Change…the Mirror will too.

Today you may
Be the Beggar,
But tomorrow,
Be the Giver.

Today, the World
Laughs at You,
But tomorrow you laugh
And the entire world
Feels encouraged and joyful!

Until this Liberation,
Visualize all success and blessings
For others,
And remain humbly aloof.

8

Bound, Hand to Neck.

Know that with your actions
You are producing the Good
Karma that will
Affect your next Birth.

Make Prayers
Of Gratitude and Thanksgiving
For having such
A wonderful opportunity.

Traveling through
Life and Death
Is our very Nature,
How we travel is our choice.

In Wisdom,
Do Virtuous Actions
Without any attachment
To Results.

Realize That,
From out of the Supreme Source
You have emerged, and into
The Supreme Source you will submerge,
But never have you been separate.

Speak for those being silenced
And defend the defenseless,
But see that you hold no resentments.

Breathe-In:
The poison of hate, anger,
And unforgiveness.

Breathe-Out:
The wish that all Beings extinguish the source of suffering,
Which is self-clinging,

And that all Beings find the source of happiness,
Which is helping others.

Grasping and envy is an illness.
Give it all away.

Anxiety and Worry are proof that
You still think you are only this body.
Give it all away.

Holding onto the Personal Self
Is like being cold, lost,
And fearful in a dark, wet Cave.

Letting go, and experiencing
The Body of Infinite Simplicity
Is like soaring through the vast, limitless Sky!

9

Pond of Beastliness

Like a Compass
Bought in a Dream,
Praise and Blame
Cannot point you
In the right direction either.

Success and Failure
Cannot be diagnosed
From the outside.

Regretting your Past
And fretting about the future
Makes the present
Opportunities inaccessible.

Practice being here until "Now" disappears,
And you dwell nowhere.

Like visiting a new city,
Explore the tiniest detail of Now.

If you can stay present
Just for few moments,
Everything becomes self-luminous.

Breath-In:

"Many will never know or see this wondrous miracle."

Breathe-Out:

"May these prayers reach all the Realms of Life
And reveal this miracle to them."

10

Chasing a Mirage

If a wrong from your past
Arises in your thoughts
Consistently during Meditation,
Get up and go make it right.

Become a Mystic Farmer
 Plowing the fields
Of old karmic debt.

Lose your fear.

See,
The Scarecrow is empty.
 Pull it apart and scatter it abroad.

Plant now the seeds of compassion and loving-kindness.

In due time, these seeds will spring up
And you will walk in a Good Harvest...
Without a shadow.

By defending your ego, you strengthen your enemy.

The weapons of destruction mightily flung at Siddhartha
Fell to the ground in a harmless rain of Flowers.

For how could they not,
His love never saw them?

Wear the Body
Of Infinite Simplicity at Dawn
And it's you
In the amber-light-electric-rain
Crackling across the New Earth.

Wear the Body of Infinite
Simplicity at Dusk,
And it's you
Appearing
From out of obscurity,
As a billion burning Suns.

The Commoner
Seeks comfort.

The Hero takes
On Pain.

Those on the Path,
Abide in what is.

Even the Great King Ashoka,
Who conquered the entire World
with Dharmic Love,
Is almost forgotten now.

Everything is in Flux.

It is moving,

Fading, disappearing,

And reappearing in new forms.

When you have given up acting,

You do not cling to the travelling show,

And you can laugh along with the audience.

By thinking only of helping others,

How can you not be helped?

Goodness

Rebounds upon you...

It always has and always will.

11

Net of Fate

Looking over this incredible Vastness,
Nowhere is there to be found
A personal "Self".

There is only Awareness.

It looks out of my eyes.
It looks out of your eyes.

It causes the entire World to feel.

Nothing would matter
If matter was nothing,
But without question,
It's really something.

Just don't ask me, "What?"

But, when you are breathing in
The clear Energy of a trillion Supernovas,
You could jump to the moon if you truly wanted to.

Reflecting on this,
Breathe into your Heart-Area.
Shake off depression and aimlessness.
Create new hope for the hopeless.

Forget your "self".
Smile and be joyful.
Never cause harm.

Gather with other Practitioners.

Try to sit comfortably
On a chair or the floor.

Cast your gaze down,
Or close your eyes.

Breathe in through your nose.
(Deeply)
Breathe out through your mouth.
(Completely)

Your awareness is your breath,
Follow it in
And out with your mind.

Think of the words,
"Breathing In" and "Breathing Out"
When performing these actions.

The Mind will wander off.
Gently bring it back to,
"Breathing In" and "Breathing Out".

This is called, "Shamatha"
Or Breathing Meditation.

Do this meditation for at least five minutes
Before Tonglen Practice:

When you are ready, visualize with the In-Breath,
"Taking in all the pain in the World, including my own."

Then visualize with the Out-Breath,
"Sending out relief and healing to the entire World including myself."

Even one attempt at doing these Practices,
Is worth a thousand years of reading,
Studying, and talking endlessly about doing practices.

But see that you don't cling to practices either.

MahaSiddha Naropa found Enlightenment after
Being slapped in the face with a shoe!

So that…with one loud bang…religion, vows, and rules
Went out the window!

12

Bee that Honey Stuck.

How fortunate!
You have been born
A human being!

You have the intelligence, time, and space
To perfect the mind.

How did you ever come in contact with the Teachings?

How Fortunate!

Amazingly, now you have the opportunity
To leap off this old wheel
Of negative thinking!

Rejoice and quickly put these practices to use,
Before darkness again clouds the mind.

Be always thinking thoughts such as,
"Where did my childhood go?"
"Where does tomorrow exist?"
What is it that is called, "I"?
"Do any of these things really exist
Outside of my thinking of them?"

It's easy to regard the
World as a Dream,
Until it rudely barges in on you!

But even if we call it,
"Real"
Who gives it, "Meaning"?

You can choose what thoughts
You foster. You can choose
What words you speak.

And by them, you
Create your World.

Fear only ignorance.
Be Awake.
Control the Dream.

When all things are fading,
You are burning bright
In Non-Duality.

Way up there among the stars,
It is the same substance as you.

Way inside the tiniest Atom,
It is the same substance as you.

So, what is this thing we are still calling
"You" and "I"?

Consider the body,
"A container."

It is condensed energy
In a massive field of energy
Of lesser density.

And,
In this Buddha-Land
Of various fields of energy
A pack of Phantom Energy-Dogs might hunt down and kill
A Phantom-Energy-Deer, a Phantom-Energy-Tsunami
Might engulf a Phantom-Energy-City
And drown its Phantom-Energy-Inhabitants,
A Phantom-Energy-Bullet might burst
 Through a Phantom-Energy-Head,
Or
Phantom-Energy-People might Make-Love with Phantom-Energy-Passion…then enjoy Phantom-Energy-Cake!

How Extraordinary!

It is equally without meaning,
And incredibly important.

13

Cow of Life

Erase from memory
"Tree"
See it again for the first time.

Erase from memory
"Person"
See them again for the first time.

Erase from memory
"Corruption"
See the World again for the first time.

Erase both
"Striving"
And
"Not Striving".

If you are an Ordained Monastic
Having taken the Sīla Vows,
You may beg your daily meal
In accordance with
The Monastic Code of Conduct.

If you are a Mahasiddha or Practitioner,
Having taken The Five Precept Vows,
Work With your hands and mind.

Be beneficial to others,
And you will lack nothing.
Do not be idle.

Find a street, park, or public restroom to Clean
as Mediation Practice.

There are worse
Things than shit and trash,
Like a haughty, ungrateful spirit.

Be kind, industrious, generous,
Helpful to others,
And you will not starve.

Flash open Your Heart.
Don't call
Attention to yourself.

Be a Child of Wonder,
Playing with generosity.

No one can even
Count the Trillions of Life-Forms
On a single Cow.

And are you
Still thinking in terms of
"My World" and "My Problems"?

Floating in a sea
Of billions of Universes,
Whatever that is,
"That" is all
We are.

It is as
Much out there,
As it is in
Here.

How amazing, that nothing is real
And nothing exists,
As such.

There is nothing that has ever been found
Anywhere,
That is actually
"Solid".

Things consist of smaller things
And those smaller things
Are made of
Even smaller
Things,
Until
Everything
Breaks down
Into Nothing.

From nothing
Comes Vibration.

From Vibration
Comes Atoms.

From Atoms
Come things.

But there is no
Such thing
As Nothing,
Anywhere.

Even that seemingly
"nothing"
In front of your face,
Is really something.

You are swimming in Mind.

Trade in all your wrongs, injustices, hurts,
And fears for mercy,
Hope, compassion, and kindness.

An open Heart is the best medicine,
Open it a little more
With every breath.

Be like a little kid, running with Wonder,
"What is this?"
"Is all this, Alive or Dead?",
"Is all this real or unreal?"

Understand,
The physical form came from the Earth
But the Earth came from the Mind.

The Body of Infinite Simplicity
Is a mixture of both and neither.

It has no fixed abode,
But can be tracked by following
A trail of signs, wonders,
And miracles.

Faithfully think upon these things.

When you do these Practices,
Stress and Worry cannot
Find You.

14

Fleeting Shadows

Drawn to that which pleases,
Repelled by that which doesn't,
And unconcerned about the rest,
Is this any way to live?

Examine how the mind
Works in this habitual way.

Turn these three distractions
Into three seeds of contemplation.

Do not chase what only pleases the self.

Do not run away from difficulties and challenges.

Try to learn from everything.

Notice that all things are interesting in their own way.

Practice giving.

Give yourself permission
To relax and be joyous.

Begin with yourself, when it comes to
Gentleness, forgiveness,
And kindness.

Everything is just happening
And not happening
All at the same time.
Enjoy it.

Nothing Exists, yet
Here it is all the Time.
Enjoy it.

Work with what
You have and don't have.

Bring everything onto
The Path of the Mind.

If you are "Pissed Off"
Be pissed on the Path
Of the Mind.

Breath-In, "I'm so pissed, right now!"
Breath-Out, "May all Beings that are pissed-off find Peace!"

When you show Progress on the Spiritual Path,
The benefit of your practice is quite simple.

You are decreasing your misery
From many lives to one,
From years to months,
From months to weeks,
From weeks to days,

From days to hours,
From hours to minutes,
From minutes to seconds,
From seconds to non-arising.

You will find that your world
Is not a dreadful hell or a magnificent heaven
...It is what it is.

What more could you ask,
From a Spiritual Practice?

Oh Great-Being,
How obsessively we think about
The occupant of this
Vacant House!

15

Rough-Coated Dogs

When problems and stress
Arise in your consciousness,
The cause is Ignorance.

Somehow you are holding onto the view,
"I am not at peace with this."

In these times,
We should remain
In a place of not knowing,
Without labeling
"Good" or "Bad."

Things are what they are,
Namely,
"Impermanent" and yet "affected by thought."

In the gap of unknowing,
Thoughts dissolve and
Everything becomes clear.

16

A Snare.

Never argue or try to convince others.

Every truth is personal, hard-won,
And comes from direct experience.

No one can walk upon the Path you are on.

No two people pray to the same God.

Even if two
Kneel together in prayer,
Their prayers go
In separate directions.

The God in one
Mind may act, speak,
And think slightly differently
Then the God in the other's Mind.

Even if the two
Agree to study
The same book
About this God,
They interpret the book
In different ways.

The God in one of the books is jealous,
Angry, grieved, and hard to please,
While the God in the other book is gentle, forgiving,
Patient, and all-accepting.

And to those on the Path of the Mind,
Any God who's emotions can be affected by
Its followers or by nonbelievers,
Is still spiritually immature,
Trapped on the Wheel of Suffering
And Subject to Birth and Death
Just as we are.

If we are told to pray to a God, Buddha, or Bodhisattva
That suffers from the same fluctuation
Of emotions, happy one day and sad the next,
What could they save us from?

For, it is by these changing emotions that we suffer and
Are never completely satisfied, ourselves.

The same mind
That is producing this fluctuation of emotions,
Cannot imagine a God without
The same fluctuation of emotions.

Thus, there is nothing
Worthy of our reverence
In Gods such as these.

Only in the Body of Infinite Simplicity
Do we begin to see the Transcendence
That is beyond all hope and fear.

To begin this journey,
Start by being grateful
For everything and to everyone,
Hands together
In prayer,
Touching the forehead.

Be overjoyed with what you
Already have and don't have,
Hands together
In prayer,
Touching the forehead.

Even with a cup of water:

Breath-In, "Because all Beings thirst, may I
Drink this for them."

Breath-Out, "May all Beings receive the refreshing affects
Of this pure, clean, water of life."

Even while working:
Breath-In, "Even though my work is hard and boring,
There are those who cannot work
And have no income, and even more
Whose work is much worse and dangerous!"

Breath-Out, "May all beings find work that
Is meaningful, beneficial to all, and keeps them in ample supply."

These visualizations are a form of play.

Make a game of strengthening
Your imagination.

Get excited about the things
You are starting to notice.

Stir up a blissful feeling and acknowledge
What a great opportunity you have to breathe out
The positive energy of change upon the World.

Be happy and grateful about your Tonglen Practice,
For by it, you are training your mind to
Carry out the work of your hands.

17

A Merciless Hunter

If you think you
Are Enlightened,
Trouble will come around
And show that you are not.

The Path of the Mind
Is not for escaping life
Or making it something
It is not.

The Path of the Mind,
Is for embracing what is.

What others call broken, displaced,
Troublesome, soiled, embarrassing, lonely,
Sick, diseased, oozing with death,
And desolate,
Of these, we do not turn away.

If these parts of ourselves are not embraced
And troubles do not come,
How boring!
What is there to learn?

Better that we find these traps, expose our ego,
And perfect our mind, than to live
In comfort, slowly slipping, falling
Into an even more painful Cycle of existence.

Only when sick,
Do you seek a cure.

Only when tired,
Do you seek rest.

Only when suffering,
Do you seek relief.

Only when poisoned,
Do you seek an antidote.

Yet, there is nothing
To figure out.

Nothing is completely
Satisfying nor not
Satisfying.

All things only appear
To begin and end,
Come together
And fall apart.

Confronting suffering, fear,
And breathing it all in,
Is what helps remind you that you are
THIS coming together
And falling apart.

There are things that are productive
And lead to happiness,
And things that are unproductive
And lead to further suffering.

See that the path you follow
Was cut by the Wise and not by a fool.

Mara is the embodiment of delusion,
It is said that he brings fearful thoughts and terror.

In the end, it is only thought,
Not gods or demons.

You are not a male or a female.
You are not a self.

There is nothing there
For Mara to scare.

Enlightenment is merely
A fancy way of saying,
That you have lost
Your Anxiety about it all.

18.

Entanglement in Bondage

Base your intentions,
Words, thoughts, actions, work,
Relationships, meditations, and World View
On Compassion and Joyfulness.

When it seems that things are
Working out for the better,
Place your hands together
In prayer, touching your forehead.

When it seems that things are
Working out for the worst,
Place your hands together
In prayer, touching your forehead.

When you have found something
Valuable or lost
Something valuable,
Place your hands together
In prayer, touching your forehead.

Do the same
When encountering
Acceptance or resistance.

Do the same
When encountering
Praise and Blame.

Do the same when
Everyone is speaking
Well of you and when you
Can't seem to please anyone.

Ask yourself,
"Do these thoughts or opinions
Really exist or am I reacting to a Phantom?"

It is like screaming at someone
For opening the door,
And then finding out
That it was
Only the Wind.

Seek the Community
Of Meditation Practitioners
For support.

19

Unsafe Footpath

To allow Compassion
To naturally flow from your
Body, speech, and mind,
Live from the Heart.

Your only strengths
Are in your determination
To awaken from this sleep,
To tame the ego, and liberate
All beings trapped under the
Crushing weight of negative thought.

Approach every act
As if it were your
Last on Earth.

Think,
"If my next birth were
Determined by this act alone,
What impact would it have,
Favorable or Unfavorable?"

"What Karmic impact
Will be left on my loved ones and
The World in general,
By this word, thought, or deed?"

And, "In the End, what will I do,
When it is made clear to me, that there
Is no one else to blame for my situation?"

Seek to make
Peace without
Judging who is
Right or wrong.

Walk away
From argument.

Heal old and new
Wounds before
They get infected.

Do not talk about people behind their back.
Quickly over look their mistakes,
As well as your own.

If you can stop from doing just these three things, you will
Have produced more positive Karmic Seeds, than are atoms
Scattered though-out the entire Universe!

At various times
And in various places,
There will be earthquakes,
Floods, famine, fire, disease,
And even collisions with astral bodies.

Such things are not to be feared…
If you are living with the thought,
"Like me, all being want to be protected,
Loved, and accepted. I will help them!"

During troubled
Times, if someone
Says, "Pray to my God
Or lose your head!"

Better to live without
A head, then to live
With one owned
By another.

Someone might say,
"Pray to our God and live
In his kingdom with us forever!"

Consider how much time you
Want to spend around
Such people?

Find your own truth.
Question everything.

20

In a Pit

The fool waits
For conditions
To be right before
Being happy.

And even then, it is fleeting.

Maintain a joyous
Attitude, always.

Be ridiculous.

Dance.
Speak to strangers.
Change your look.
Change your name.
Change the subject.

Be still.
Move.

Be happy for no apparent reason.

Gossip about good things.

Lend a hand.

Practice your meditation in the noisiest,
Dirtiest, most populated spot,
Breathing-In, "Escaping the World."
Breathing-Out, "Embracing the World."

If you abandon
The city for
A mountain cave,
You will soon discover
That the screaming sirens,
Barking dogs,
And loud music,
Were not really
The cause of your distraction.

Open welcoming arms to the World,
Let it in.
Invite it to your meditation,
And it will not disturb you.

A cry, a kiss, a book, the wind,
The smell of coffee and eggs,
A bird, a cat, a cloud,
A walk in the park, these are
Magical things, too extraordinary
To mention!

All things are by nature, happy.

It is Illusionary Suffering that says, "There is no comfort
Here, only change."

It is Illusionary Impermanence that says, "There is no stability
Here, only change."

It is Illusionary Death that says, "There is no staying
Here, only change."

But, the Wisdom of Emptiness & Compassion says,
"There is no one who wrote this,
 No one reading this,
Nor anything to be read,
And yet here it is,
Deal with it."

Oh Seeker, if you listen to silence,
Everything is being said at once.

So, practice being quiet.

Practice being still.

It is better to not have an answer,
But if you must, make it
A life-affirming one.

It is better to not have an opinion,
But if you must, make it
A life-affirming one.

Better to not teach,
But if you must,
Teach joyfulness and compassion.

Better to not make a decision,
But if you must, make sure
That it is beneficial to all.

21

Spear tip beating on drum

Intoxicants cloud the mind,
So that you will
Never understand.

If you are doing something,
That must be hidden,
Stop.

Harm no living thing.
 Speak the Truth.
Do not take what is not given you.
Avoid sexual misconduct.
Do away with cheating, and harmful speech.

Siddhartha is our Role-Model.
Look to his many Teachings for direction.

Go to the assembly of Meditation Practitioners for encouragement.
If you cannot find an assembly, create one.

Do what needs
To be done
Without seeking
Results.

Work with whatever
Arises spontaneously.

Do the next right thing,
And your life will be sweet incense.

Have pure motivation,
And your life will be a Light for all to see.

Be sincere.
Live according to your true nature.

It is better to be a sincere Fool,
Than to fake that you are wise.

People can be helped
By the truth of your brokenness,
But not by the lie of your wholeness.

22

Fragile-Water Plant

The moment before Enlightenment,
Siddhartha gently touched
The Earth with hand.

So too, should you
Live close to the ground.

Be careful what you eat,
Drink, and apply to the body.

Evil kings think nothing
Of poisoning their own kingdom
For profit.

Eat only what
Naturally comes
From Earth's body.

Drink only what
Naturally comes
From Earth's breast.

As non-virtuous actions
Lead to suffering,
Not listening to the
Earth leads only to misery.

23

Snake-Conquering

Surprise yourself
By being unpredictable
And trustworthy.

Change your style of clothes.
Change your look.
Grow a beard.
Shave your beard.
Grow your hair long.
Cut it all off.
Join a group.
Quit a group.
Go down different streets.
Talk to different people.
Learn a trade.
Learn an instrument.
Learn a silly game.
Do something different.
Do the opposite of what you have normally done.
Walk out of town.
Come back to town.
Call your father and mother.
Stop calling your father and mother so much.
Disappear or reappear.
Forget everything you know about yourself.
Start again, knowing nothing.

Practice never saying
Another negative thing
About yourself, people,
Places, things, and
Even the weather.

Be honest
Even when dealing
With someone that
Doesn't like you.

Warn others of traps,
Even if they
Won't listen.

People learn from
Mistakes,
But help them
Get back up
When they fall.

24.

Sharpened Fangs

In Tibet, there is an ancient practice.
It is performed only by true, spiritual seekers.

He or she goes out alone,
Into a desolate,
Isolated wilderness.

There is no help for miles around,
And wolves hide in the darkness.

The Spiritual Seeker cries out,
Beating a small drum, and blowing
A trumpet specially made for this ritual.

They scream out in agony,
Inviting the demons of Pride,
The demons of Lust, and the demons
Of Stupidity to come and make
A meal of their flesh, drink their blood,
And chew on their bones until
There is nothing left.

Many Tibetans believe
That this is the ultimate way
Of giving absolutely everything you have
In payment for past negative, karmic deeds.

These Seekers risk illness, madness,
And even death by fright,
To confront their worst fears,
And rid themselves, once and for all,
From these imaginary, Mind-Produced Enemies.

Those who have emerged
From such battles with themselves,
Have realized the non-reality and lack of substance
Behind pride, anger, lust, and stupidity.

These Seekers have even lost their belief
In demons, death, and a personal Self.

They have entered Into the Inconceivable Vastness
Of the Body of Infinite Simplicity,
All that there is or ever will be.

Oh Seeker, there are two kinds of Suffering.

One type of Suffering is Temporary,
It requires facing your fears and trying something different.
This is the Suffering that leads to the end of Suffering.

The other type of Suffering,
Is from being afraid, remaining stuck, and not trying to learn.
This is the Suffering that leads only to more Suffering.

25

Moon In Water

Oh Perfect-Being,
Accept whatever hardships
Befall you, but wish only
Success for others.

At least, learn to hold your tongue,
And say nothing until
The drama passes.

Don't say what
Can't be taken back.

Don't put in motion
What can't be stopped.

Don't go out of your way
To be cruel, causing
Physical or Emotional injury.

Seek peace and forgiveness quickly.
Make amends swiftly.
Take a little insult with Humor.

If you must look around
Before saying or doing something,
Don't do it.

Let others roll around
In the folly of
"I'm better than you."

Ask yourself,
"How does it feel...
To be looked down upon in judgment...
With a sneer or a glare?"

Then, be a friend, even to your enemies.

Lift them up and
Let karma run its course.

Trying to be first,
We push others down
And trip over them.

Be the first one to help serve,
And the last one to eat.

Smile, even without teeth.

Let it be said of you,
"Never have I heard them say
An unkind word about anybody!"

Let people gossip
About your good works.

No one is completely loved.
No one is completely hated.

Your enemy is someone's child,
Parent, lover, and friend.

Like-wise,
Your Best friend is someone's
Worst enemy.

There is nothing that is happening
To you right now,
That isn't common to all.

Pray for those in your situation,
And those that have it worse.

Be true to your Teacher,
Siddhartha,
The Teaching of the Way,
And to the Community of Practitioners.

If you are right,
Stand by it.

If you are wrong,
Admit it.

Don't be afraid to take
A risk on something new.

See it all,
As experiments
On the Path
Of the Mind.

26

Bubble of Bewilderment

Cracked, festering skin, a disfigured face,
Twisted body, afflicted eyes, broken teeth,
An oddly shaped head and mental illness
Is no handicap
Compared to a closed mind.

If you seek success
By taking more than you need,
Put it away.

If you seek success
While ignoring the suffering of others,
Put it away.

If you seek success
By taking life, stealing, lying,
Cheating, or harming the Earth,
Put it away.

Better to starve,
Then to eat the poisonous fruit
Of these Karmic Seeds…life after life.

Before making a decision,
Ask yourself, "Does this action lead
To more suffering or to the end of suffering?"

And again,
"Will this action help lead
All beings, including myself,
To ultimate Happiness?"

See yourself
In others.

Lead a life of Wisdom,
Compassion, purpose, and devotion.

See the good
In all things.

Be grateful,
To everyone.

Is there a better alternative?

27

Fleeting Mist

You alone, can right all wrongs.

You alone, can feed and clothe the needy.

You alone, can bring healing to the sick.

You alone, can protect the battered women and children.

You alone, can bring rain to parched lands.

You alone, can cause flowers to grow in desolate places.

How are these mighty deeds accomplished?

Let these things ride your breath and fill your mind.

Bring in this hot drought with the In-Breath,

Bring forth the cool rains with your Out-Breath.

Bring in the lost, lonely, sad, and hurting with your In-Breath.

Bring forth love, compassion, health, aid, food, drink,

And hope with your Out-Breath.

Give them all your thought-energy

And your physical energy.

One day,

You will even give away your own body.

As you eat,

So too, will you be eaten.

Even if your body
Is burned to ashes
And kept in an impenetrable box,
Eventually, you will be swallowed up
By the Source.

Yet,
Where are you to go
In this gone-gone-beyond-gone-
Still-here-ness?

It's tricky to say…
You know anything.

Buddha said that he knew nothing
But Suffering, and the Path
That leads to the end of Suffering,
And the World made him
Into a Wooden Statue to
Be put up on a shelf and forgotten.

But what is wood,
Is it not a billion sparkling particles
Filled with Buddha-Nature?

And what are you made from,
A billion sparkling particles?

What does that make you, a wooden statue
Or a Buddha?

28.

Rippling Water

Begin your day with leisure.
Clear your bowels.
Brush your teeth.
Wash the body.
Eat.

Sit down.
Close the eyes or cast an unfocused gaze
Straight ahead and down.

Sit for as long as you can
With the thought,
"Breathing In, Breathing Out."
(Shamatha Meditation.)

Open your eyes and tell yourself,
"Today I will do Tonglen Meditation
For all Beings and whatever arises
On my path."

Stand up and stretch if you are able.

Go about your day.

And when retiring at night,
Again,
Sit quietly.
Reflect on your day.

Were you kind to all Beings?
What could you have done better?

Did you do Tonglen?
Could you have done better?

Smile, now.
Relax.
It is alright.
Let your thoughts subside.

Remember, regardless
Of your idea of how well you did,
You will always be
That mysterious Substance
Of which, the entire Universe
Is made.

Now, close the eyes again
Or cast an unfocused gaze
Straight ahead and down.

Return, for a time, to
"Breathing In and Breathing Out."

Get some rest now.

Wherever you are
You are
One.

29

Old Age, Sickness, and Death

Do not get bloated with pride
When things seem to go right for you.

Do not hang your head and complain
When things seem to go wrong.

What business is it of yours?

Who are you?

Who is this happening to?

What you are feeling, is a trick of all tricks.

When the 84 thousand cells
Perceive something in unison,
There arises a false sense of "Self."

It is a feeling of wholeness,
In what is actually Interdependent-Separateness.

It is not by sheer accident,
That there is this feeling
Of a Ghost
In the Machine.

It is an amazing feat,
Performed by an amazing organism.

All the wise sages
In all the worlds,
Could not have dreamed up
A body such as this!

And yet, what is dreaming what?

The Cells can be said to be dreaming the "mind."

And the mind can be said to be dreaming the body.

But what is dreaming the Cells...
When there
Is nothing to be found in them but Mind?

People of ancient times,
Because they did not know
 Cells feel everything simultaneously,
Called this phenomenon, "Soul",
"Spirit", "Ego", "Self", "Awareness,"
Or "Consciousness."

It's also described as "Me", "Myself", and "I".

For, what are you thinking of,
When you point at the body
And say, "I know"?

Are you thinking of this bloody sack of puke,
Crap, meat, bones, hair, farts, ear wax, boogers, and brains?

Do you think you own this body?

Do you think you will never part from this body?

I tell you,
When the cells in one part of the body die,
You quickly tell the doctor to remove that part
And throw it away
As if it didn't even belong to you!

So, don't hang on
To thoughts like,
"This is mine" and "This I am."

Neither will last.
Let go.
Laugh.

You are a walking corpse,
Falling apart.

Give it all away.

Even Siddhartha made mistakes in thinking.

He once thought that starving
The body would lead to enlightenment.

But because the 84 thousand cells want to live,
It only strengthened the Ego!

He realized that you must supply the body
With what it needs, so that you
Will have some freedom
From desire.

Then you can contemplate,
"What is that which
is Deathless?"

A living teacher can get you close.
Siddhartha can get you close.
The Teachings can get you close.
The Company of Practitioners can get you close.

But in the end, it was not Buddha
Holding up the flower that caused the Monk
To smile and Awaken that day.

Perhaps,
The Monk saw an indescribable event
Happening in space, caused by innumerable
Actions and reactions, going back throughout infinite time…

Emanating from some type of Energy Awareness
In the form of our own thoughts.

THIS, Indescribable Force…
Was the Teacher,
Was the Flower, was the Monk…
And their Shadows!

When you enter the gap
 Between thoughts, new ways
Of seeing are born.

But, others say...
It was just a simple flower
Holding Buddha up
So that a White Oleander Blossom
Could smile and Awaken, that day.

Clear your Mind of intoxicants
And your body of poisons.

Find other practitioners.
Live on the Earth.
Drink in the Sun.

Escape old thinking patterns.
Stretch the Yogic Body.

Be on the move.

Seek the end of ignorance.

Use your life wisely, helping others.

Practice Shamatha and Tonglen with every breath.

These Karminc Seeds will bring you all the food,
Friends, and freedom you will ever need.

The cells in the head think,
But the cells in the Heart, know.

The body is a vehicle.
Listen to the Heart in Silence.
Learn its voice.

Quieting the false sense of self,
You will hear the Heart singing
Wisdom-Songs.

Breath-In: your timidity and fear.
Breath-Out: the courage to live life whole heartedly.

Whatever you can't let go, let it go.

Work with whatever spins around in your mind endlessly.
See your thoughts as the powerless, unreal phantoms that there are.

That, which hurts, that which angers,
That which confuses, scares, intimidates, frustrates,
Bores, or makes happy, put them on the Path of the Mind.

Pull them apart,
And dissect them.

See the unreality of their nature.

They are nothing.
They can't hurt you,
Only thoughts…Only thoughts.

30.

On a Razor Blade

Neither Success nor Failure,
Neither Praise nor Blame, define you.

Keep moving forward.

Life is more than what
You wear, where
You stay, and what
You have.

Do what is right,
Stay sober and vigilant.
Reach out to others for help
And be of help to others.

Watch your mind
And Practice always.

Devote your life to whatever brings liberation.

Find your own truth,
Not the truth of others.

Relax.
Be cool.
Smile.

Your entire life
Is the Path of Awakening.

Get excited about being
Beneficial to others.

This leads to the
Body of Infinite Simplicity
That survives even Death.

31

Poisonous Leaves

Link all your Priorities
To Compassion.

Above all
Have joy.

There will
Be growing pains.

One day you will act
Like a Saint,
The next,
A most retched
Bastard.

Don't give-up your practice,
Even if people think
You are crazy.

Don't give-up your practice,
Even if you think
You are crazy.

When a Perfect-Being,
Is given a chance to smile
With complete compassion
On another that is suffering,

They will even risk being lost
For Eons in tormenting hells.

And yet,
You sigh so loudly
And roll your eyes
Over the smallest, little thing!

Have a little faith in others,
They are struggling
And want happiness like you.

Have a little faith in
Your purpose and practice.

With patience
And persistence,
You will gain understanding.

32

Seek Out the Guru

Work with your hands.
Be useful to others, meditate,
Be quiet, loving, and strong.

Make an effort
To do good
In secret.

When people applaud,
Don't believe it.

When people hiss,
Don't believe
This either.

Be a Teacher
Of Truth...
By listening deeply
To the Truths of others,
And honoring them.

What excitement
To just breathe!
You will not always
Have this ability,
Use it for Tonglen,
Shamatha, and well doing.

The Body of Infinite Simplicity
Is likened unto
The vibrating energy
Called "Water" that is being
Displaced by the vibrating
Energy called, "Fish."

Look around at your own predicament.

There is no empty space anywhere.

There has never
Been a place where nothing
Exists, nor a place
Where anything can be found, except
Empty space.

We should have come
To realize by now,
That never has there been a reason
To worry about anything, ever.

Life and Death
Are in the thoughts you nourish.

So, Think Well.

Do not settle for being a fast
Moving river,
Where no one dares to swim.

A river that is contaminated,
Full of rotting limbs,
Fish hooks on strong lines,
Treacherous currents, deadly undertows
And evil whirlpools.

You are the Body of Infinite Simplicity:
The Buddha-Nature,
Manifesting and shining
In the form of kindness, friendliness,
Compassion, love, joy, and serenity.

You are the Ocean of Spiritual Bliss,
Pure, blue, vast and golden.

All things live in you,
And are nourished by you.

The more you help, the more help arrives.
The more you love, the more love arrives.
The more you give, the more is shared.

Oh, Seeker!
Dam-up the sickly river,
So that an Ocean of Divinity
Can flow through your spirit…
Into all the Worlds and beyond!

There is no mystery
In the Wisdom,
"Die before you die."

In that void,
When the ego is gone,
All things
Become a reservoir of joy.

Look within and listen…

The sound of the Universe
Is in every breath…

But that which makes
The Sound and hears
The Sound…is the same…
It is the Supreme Source…
Playing a delightful game.

Showing Compassion could not get any easier,

Just find this book online, then the Name & Address of a local Homeless Shelter in your area, and order as many copies as you can using this shelter's Name & Mailing Address for delivery purposes.

Snap, you have just donated books and shared the Dharma, anonymously!

Please do this, and email or write us telling where you sent them...so we can mark that one off our list of "books needed here!"

-Contact-

HMP Street Dharma

P.O. Box 71

Floresville, Texas 78114

Email: hmpstreetdharma@gmail.com

Website: hmpstreetdharma.org

DISCLAIMER:

I am blessed to have been a small part of the writing of this text...and I am trying to live its message myself.

I would not be a good leader, teacher, or guru for you. I have, however, had some success organizing meditation groups in homeless shelters...and can definitely support and guide your efforts in starting a Homeless Meditation Practitioner's group in your area. (Contact info above.)

For further research on the Ancient Spiritual Tradition of Going Forth into Homelessness,

I suggest reading about "Sramanas, Mahasiddhas, Renouncers, Homeless Sadhus of India, Yogis, Hermits, Ngakpas, Jain Siddhas, Buddhist Monks & Nuns, monasticism, Christ Jesus, Ascetics, Crazy Wisdom, Mahamudra, Dzochen, Siddhārtha Gautama, Buddha, Great Sages, Ramana Maharshi, Ramesh Balsekar, and my own Lama, **Tulku Tsori Rinpoche**.

Big Love. –kjc

Made in the USA
San Bernardino, CA
21 January 2016